IN THE ZONE

VOLLEYBALL

NATASHA EVDOKIMOFF

MEDIA ENHANCED BOOKS
AV²
BY WEIGL
ADDED VALUE • AUDIO VISUAL

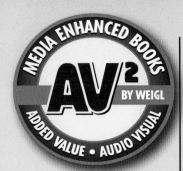

AV² by Weigl brings you media enhanced books that support active learning.

AV² provides enriched content that supplements and complements this book. Weigl's AV² books strive to create inspired learning and engage young minds for a total learning experience.

Go to **www.av2books.com**, and enter this book's unique code. You will have access to video, audio, web links, quizzes, a slide show, and activities.

BOOK CODE

H752505

Audio
Listen to sections of the book read aloud.

Video
Watch informative video clips.

Web Link
Find research sites and play interactive games.

Try This!
Complete activities and hands-on experiments.

Due to the dynamic nature of the Internet, some of the URLs and activities provided as part of AV² by Weigl may have changed or ceased to exist. AV² by Weigl accepts no responsibility for any such changes. All media enhanced books are regularly monitored to update addresses and sites in a timely manner. Contact AV² by Weigl at 1-866-649-3445 or av2books@weigl.com with any questions, comments, or feedback.

Published by AV² by Weigl
350 5th Avenue, 59th Floor
New York, NY 10118
Website: www.av2books.com www.weigl.com

Library of Congress Cataloging-in-Publication Data

Evdokimoff, Natasha.
 Volleyball : in the zone / Natasha Evdokimoff.
   p. cm.
 Includes index.
 ISBN 978-1-60596-907-7 (hard cover : alk. paper) -- ISBN 978-1-60596-908-4 (soft cover : alk. paper) --
ISBN 978-1-60596-909-1 (e-book)
 1. Volleyball--Juvenile literature. I. Title.
 GV1015.34.E93 2011
 796.325--dc22
                          2009050269

Printed in the United States of America in North Mankato, Minnesota
1 2 3 4 5 6 7 8 9 14 13 12 11 10

052010
WEP264000

PROJECT COORDINATOR Heather C. Hudak   **DESIGN** Terry Paulhus

CONTENTS

What is **Volleyball?**

Today, more than 46 million people play volleyball in the United States.

Volleyball was invented by William Morgan in 1895. During a trial game, someone said that the ball was "volleyed" over the net. The game then became known as volleyball. The first game was played at Massachusetts College in 1896. For the first few years, players used a basketball. By 1900, a special ball was designed just for volleyball.

In 1930, the first official outdoor game was played. Outdoor volleyball can be played on grass, but it is most often played on sand. Beach volleyball has developed its own rules and leagues.

In volleyball, two teams of six stand on opposite sides of a raised net. Players keep a ball in the air by hitting or passing it. Most often the ball is hit with hands, wrists, or arms. To score, a team must get the ball to touch the ground on the other side of the net within the boundary lines. Volleyball has leagues for men and women at all levels. Different rules sometimes apply to different leagues. More than 800 million people play this sport around the world every week!

By 1900, volleyball was a popular sport for both men and women.

A volleyball player's uniform must be light so the player can jump and move fast. It does not take much equipment to play volleyball.

Players usually wear T-shirts. Some players like to wear long sleeves to cushion their arms. Team members all wear the same color. Every player wears a number so the officials can make calls easily.

Players often wear a pair of gym shorts to play. They are comfortable so players can move quickly and easily.

Players wear pads on their knees and sometimes on their elbows. Pads help to prevent injuries when players dive on the floor for the ball.

A pair of good sneakers is important for this game. Sneakers have rubber soles to help prevent slipping when players jump and move for the ball.

A volleyball is made of soft, padded leather. The leather is stitched over rubber, and the ball is filled with air. The ball is very light, so hitting it with arms and wrists does not hurt. Volleyballs are usually white, but can be brightly colored for beach games.

■ A volleyball weighs between 9 and 10 ounces (255 and 283 grams).

A net separates the two teams. A volleyball net is made of **mesh**. The corners are tied to poles to pull the net tight. For adult players, the net is more than 7 feet (2.1 meters) high. For junior players, it stands just below 7 feet (2.1 m). Two flexible rods called **antennas** stick up at both ends of the net. These rods help show if the ball goes out of bounds while going over the net.

■ In volleyball, players sometimes tip the ball over the net. This tricky move can often score points.

The Court

Volleyball is played on a rectangular court. Boundary lines around the court show its area. The boundary lines are called side lines and end lines. To score a point, the ball must land inside the boundary. The area outside the boundary is called the **free zone**. If the ball lands in the free zone, it is out of play. Only the **serving** team can score points.

Both indoor and outdoor volleyball courts are the same size. Volleyball courts are 59 feet (18 meters) long by 29 feet, six inches (9 m) wide.

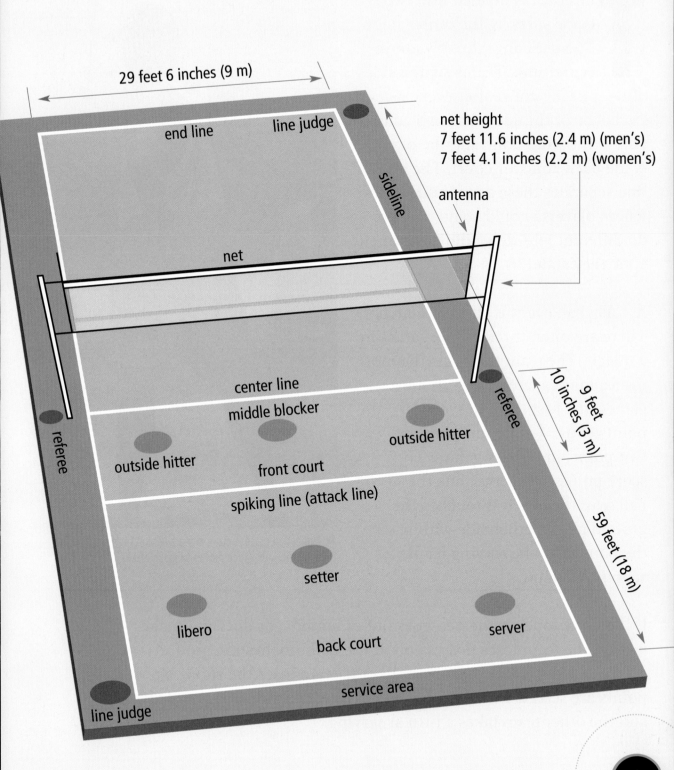

29 feet 6 inches (9 m)

end line

line judge

net height
7 feet 11.6 inches (2.4 m) (men's)
7 feet 4.1 inches (2.2 m) (women's)

sideline

antenna

net

center line

middle blocker

outside hitter

referee

9 feet
10 inches (3 m)

outside hitter

front court

spiking line (attack line)

59 feet (18 m)

referee

setter

libero

server

back court

service area

line judge

The court is divided into two equal sides by the center line. The net hangs directly above center line. Teams switch sides of the playing court after every game. Each side of the court has two zones. One is the **front zone** and the other is the **back zone**, or court. The **attack line** separates these zones and shows where players should stand. Players do different jobs depending on which zone they stand in.

A volleyball event is called a **match**. There are often three or five games in a match. The team that wins the most games in the match wins. In most games, the first team to score 15 points wins. A team must win by two points in regular games. To score points, the server hits the ball over the net. If it touches the ground on the other side within the boundary, the serving team scores one point.

Volleyball players make signals behind their back to tell their teammates which moves to make on the court.

If the serve touches the net, goes out of bounds, or does not make it over, the team loses possession. If the ball touches the ground on the serving team's side in a **rally**, the team loses the serve. No points are scored when this happens. Instead, a **side out** is called, and the other team takes a turn at serving.

Teams can hit the ball only three times when it is on their side. Players must send the ball back over the net by the third hit. A player cannot hit the ball twice in a row. Players could originally hit the ball only with their upper bodies. A 1996 rule change made it legal to play the ball off the players' lower bodies.

Not all leagues follow this ruling. If a player briefly catches or **carries** the ball, it is called a **fault**. Some other faults are reaching over the net, crossing the center line, and touching the net. If the serving team faults, it loses the serve. If the receiving team faults, it gets a point scored against them.

■ Teammates must position the ball for each other to get it over the net, because the same player cannot touch the ball twice in a row. This requires a great deal of teamwork.

Every match has two referees and two line judges. The first referee sits on a raised platform at one end of the net. This gives him or her a clear view of the entire court. The second referee stands on the floor at the other end of the net to watch for low violations.

Referees make sure the game rules are followed. The line judges stand in the free zone on opposite ends and sides of the court. Their job is to decide if the ball lands in or out of bounds. Line judges use flags to show their calls.

■ Diving for the ball is one way players try to stop the other team from scoring.

Positions

Teams are made up of six players who stand in two rows. Three stand in the front zone, and three stand in the back zone.

Players in the front zone jump at the net to **block** hard hits. They also **spike** the ball onto the other team's side. Back zone players receive serves from the other team. They also **bump** the ball to front zone players, who then try to score.

The server stands at the back of the court, usually to the right. The server steps behind the end line with the ball. He or she then hits the ball overhand or underhand over the net. This means using the hand to hit the top or bottom of the ball. If the server steps over the line, the referee calls a foot foul, and the team loses its serve. Once the ball is served, the player can step back in bounds.

■ Players serve by tossing the ball in the air with one hand and hitting it with the other hand.

■ The three front-court players try to "block," or stop, spiked balls from crossing the net. Some blockers reach well over the net and into the opponent's court.

Team members pass the ball between each other as they like, up to three times. A **set** is when a player passes the ball lightly off his or her fingertips to another team member. With this move, the ball can be pushed high in the air. A set is also called a volley. A bump is bounced off a player's extended forearms. Bumps are best to pass low balls or return hard serves or spikes.

Liberos are substitute players. They can pass and dig up hits, but they cannot jump at the net. They are strictly defensive players.

Unlike other athletes, most volleyball players play every position. Teams **rotate** positions in a clockwise direction on the court. They rotate whenever the team gets a new turn to serve.

■ The outside hitter stands on either the right or the left side of the court. The setter sets up the outside hitter. A good set allows the outside hitter to spike fast and well.

Volleyball teams start at the junior high or high school level. There are girls' and boys' teams in grades seven through twelve. Schools play against each other through the season, competing for the city title.

There are many regional volleyball clubs for young players. Club leagues have teams for girls and boys between seven and eighteen years old. There, players learn the skills they will need for highly competitive play. After high school, many players choose to play on college or university teams. These games are fast paced and fun to watch. Colleges and universities from across the country compete for the national college title.

■ One of the oldest and most important Fédération Internationale de Volleyball (FIVB) events is the Volleyball World Championship. Helena Havelkova of Czech Republic helped save the ball during a qualification game in July 2009.

Playing volleyball outside has been popular for many years. Outdoor games got started in California and were often played on the beach. Groups of people would make teams and enjoy the game as part of a fun day outside. Soon, beach games became competitive.

At first, the same rules were used for both indoor and outdoor games. Before long, beach volleyball started a separate league with its own rules. In most beach games, there are only two players per team playing on a sand court. Two-person teams guarantee the action will be fast and exciting.

All serious players would love to represent their country on an Olympic volleyball team. Both indoor and beach volleyball are played at the Summer Olympic Games. Teams from around the world play intense matches in competition for the gold medal.

Volleyball players spend many hours practicing to become good at the sport.

Professional teams get paid to play volleyball. Beach volleyball has professional men's and women's teams. The United States has a professional indoor volleyball league as well.

Beach volleyball players wear bathing suits and other stretchy clothes to help keep sand off. Because they are in the sun, players often wear sunglasses or visors. Courts are made with soft sand, so no shoes or pads are needed. Today there are professional beach volleyball leagues all over the world. Players earn prize money for winning games.

Success in international competitions, such as the Olympics, is a major accomplishment. At the 2008 Olympics, the United States won a gold medal in men's indoor volleyball. Team members spend years preparing for this level of play.

These are some of the well-known players of this exciting sport.

Karch Kiraly

LEAGUE: Professional Men's Indoor and Beach Volleyball

CAREER FACTS:

- In 1984, Kiraly was the youngest member of the men's Olympic indoor volleyball team.
- Kiraly was the Olympic indoor team captain in 1988. The team won the gold medal. With Kiraly's help the indoor team won two more gold medals, making Kiraly the only player in Olympic volleyball history to win three gold medals.
- In 1991, Kiraly was named the World Championship Most Valuable Player.
- Kiraly was named the Association of Volleyball Professionals (AVP) Most Valuable Player in 1990, 1992–1995, and 1998.
- In 1996, Kiraly won Olympic gold in the beach volleyball competition.
- Kiraly won more tournaments and money than any other player on the AVP Pro Beach tour in his 27 seasons. He won more than 3.1 million dollars playing beach volleyball.
- Kiraly was inducted into the Volleyball Hall of Fame in 2001.
- Kiraly won the AVP Outstanding Achievement Award in 2004.
- Kiraly retired from volleyball in 2007.

Sinjin Smith

LEAGUE: Professional Men's Beach Volleyball

CAREER FACTS:

- Smith played beach volleyball at UCLA. With Smith's help, UCLA won two national championships in 1976 and 1979.
- Smith has competed in more beach volleyball events than any other player. He has won the second highest number of professional beach volleyball games, behind Karch Kiraly.
- Smith was on the U.S. National Team from 1979 to 1982.
- Smith was named the AVP Best Defensive Player in 1990, 1991, and 1992.
- Smith and partner Randy Stoklos were Fédération International de Volleyball (FIVB) Tour Champions in 1989, 1990, 1991, and 1992.
- Smith was inducted into the Volleyball Hall of Fame in 2003.
- Smith retired in 2001 and is now on the board of Big Brothers of America and is president of the FIVB World Beach Council.

Flo "Flora" Hyman

LEAGUE: Professional Women's Indoor Volleyball

CAREER FACTS:

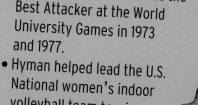

- Hyman was a three-time All-American at the University of Houston from 1974 to 1976.
- She was 6 feet (1.8 m) tall by the age of 12, and her full height as an adult was 6 foot 5 inches (1.9 m).
- Hyman was picked as All World and as the Most Valuable Player in many international tournaments.
- She was chosen to be on many All-Star Teams.
- Hyman was named as the Best Attacker in 1975, 1979, and 1983, at the Pan-Am Games.
- Hyman was also named as the Best Attacker at the World University Games in 1973 and 1977.
- Hyman helped lead the U.S. National women's indoor volleyball team to win a silver medal at the 1984 Olympic Games in Los Angeles.
- Hyman has been awarded many honors since her death in 1986, including being inducted to the Volleyball Hall of Fame in 1988.
- Since 1987, the Women's Sports Foundation has offered an award called the Flo Hyman Award for excellence in volleyball.

Gabrielle Reece

LEAGUE: Professional Women's Beach Volleyball

CAREER FACTS:

- Reece attended Florida State University, where she set the university record for most blocks, with 747.
- Reece was the leader in game **"kills"** for the 1994 to 1996 seasons.
- In 1994 and 1995, Reece was the Offensive Player of the Year.
- Reece was captain of her team for five seasons.
- Reece now works as a fashion model and television announcer.

Superstars of Today

Many athletes today are rising stars on the volleyball court.

Misty May-Treanor

LEAGUE: Professional Women's Beach Volleyball

CAREER FACTS:

- May-Treanor played volleyball at California State Long Beach from 1995 to 1999.
- In 1997 and 1998, May-Treanor won NCAA Division I First Team All-American and NCAA Player of the Year. She was inducted to the Long Beach State Athletics Hall of Fame in 2004.
- In 2000, May-Treanor was voted as one of the top six volleyball players in NCAA history.
- In 2003, May-Treanor began playing with Kerri Walsh in the Association of Volleyball Professionals (AVP) Volleyball Tour. They were voted "Best Team" in 2003, after a 9 to 0 season. They received the same honor for the next three years.
- May-Treanor was voted the AVP Best Offensive Player from 2004–2008, the AVP Best Defensive Player in 2008, and FIVB Best Setter in 2005.
- At the 2008 Olympics in Beijing, May-Treanor and Kerri Walsh won a gold medal in women's beach volleyball.

Kerri Walsh

LEAGUE: Professional Women's Beach Volleyball

CAREER FACTS:

- Walsh played volleyball at Stanford University, where she helped win national titles in 1996 and 1997.
- Walsh was a four-time All-American during her time at Stanford.
- Walsh was considered to be one of the top all-around players in college volleyball. She had 1,553 kills, 1,285 digs, and 502 blocks during her time at Stanford.
- At the 2004 Olympics in Athens, Walsh and May-Treanor won gold in women's beach volleyball. They won every game at the 2004 Olympics.
- Walsh enjoyed a winning streak of 89 matches from 2003 to 2004.
- Walsh was a two-time AVP Most Valuable Player in 2003 and 2004.
- Walsh led the AVP in both blocks and hitting percentage from 2005 to 2007.
- At the 2008 Olympics in Beijing, Misty and Walsh won a gold medal in women's beach volleyball.
- Walsh is married to Casey Jennings. Casey is one of the best men's volleyball players in the world.

Logan Tom

LEAGUE: Professional Women's Indoor and Beach Volleyball

CAREER FACTS:

- Tom was a four-time All-American at Stanford University. She was named NCAA Most Valuable Player in 2001.
- Tom was the youngest player picked for the U.S. National Team in 1996.
- Tom was only 19 when she played in the 2000 Olympics in Sydney, Australia.
- Tom was named NCAA Stanford Regional Most Outstanding Player in 2001 and 2002.
- With Tom's help, the U.S. National Team placed fifth at the 2004 Olympics in Athens.
- Tom was named beach volleyball AVP Rookie of the Year in 2006.
- Tom helped her team win silver in women's indoor volleyball at the 2008 Olympics in Beijing, and she was named Best Scorer of the 2008 Olympic games.
- In September 2008, Tom announced that she had joined Hisamitsu Springs, a women's indoor volleyball team in Japan.

Todd Rogers

LEAGUE: Professional Men's Beach Volleyball

CAREER FACTS:

- Rogers attended University of California Santa Barbara, where he was an All-American in 1995 and 1996.
- Rogers first began competing professionally in beach volleyball in 1995.
- Rogers was voted AVP Rookie of the Year in 1997.
- Rogers began playing with Phil Dalhausser in 2006. They have been voted AVP Team of the Year in 2007 and 2008.
- Rogers was named FIVB Best Defensive Player in 2006, 2007, and 2008.

- Rogers and Dalhausser won gold in men's beach volleyball at the 2008 Olympics in Beijing.
- Rogers and Dalhausser won the AVP Crocs Cup in 2007, 2008, and 2009.

Staying Healthy

A healthy diet helps people be strong athletes. Fruits and vegetables provide many of the vitamins people need. Breads, pasta, and rice are sources of food energy. Meats have protein for building muscles. Dairy products have calcium, which keeps bones strong. Eating foods from all the food groups everyday will keep a player's body in top condition.

Drinking plenty of water before, during, and after playing sports is important. Water keeps people's bodies cool and running well. When athletes sweat, they lose water. Water replaces what is lost through sweat during a game.

■ Drinking plenty of water before, during, and after playing sports is important.

■ Pasta is a good source of carbohydrates. Carbohydrates provide the body much of the energy it needs to keep active and healthy.

Strong and flexible muscles are important for playing well. Training the right muscles a few times every week makes playing more fun and helps prevent injuries. Stretching keeps muscles flexible. It is best to stretch after a **warmup**. Running in place for a few minutes or doing some laps gets muscles warm.

Strong legs are needed for quick movements. For strong legs, players practice jumping in place. They pull their knees up as high as they can on each jump. Lunges are other great exercises for stretching leg muscles. Standing with their feet slightly apart, players shift their weight to one side and bend their knee. The other leg stays straight and stretches out.

Players need strong hands and fingers, too. To work these muscles, they squeeze a tennis ball in each hand several times. Players also stretch their shoulder muscles to prepare for hitting and passing the ball.

It is important to always be careful when stretching to avoid pulling muscles.

Volleyball Brain Teasers

Test your knowledge of this exciting sport by trying to answer these volleyball brain teasers!

1 What is the position of the player who starts the action in a volleyball game?

2 What is the name of the move where a player bounces the ball off their forearms?

3 What kind of ball was first used to play volleyball?

4 How many times may the volleyball be hit on one side of the court before it must be hit back over the net to the other team?

5 What is the name of the move where a player pushes the ball up into the air for other players to hit or pass?

6 What do some players do as a last chance to get the ball?

ANSWERS: 1. The position of the player who starts the action in a volleyball game is the server. 2. The move where a player bounces the ball off their forearms is called a bump, or forearm pass. 3. The first kind of ball used to play volleyball was a basketball. By 1900, a special ball was designed just for volleyball. 4. A volleyball may be hit three times before it must be hit back over the net to the other team. The same player may not hit the ball twice in a row. 5. When a player pushes the ball up into the air for other players to hit or pass, this is called a set. A good set can often make for a good spike. 6. Some players dive, especially in beach volleyball, as a last chance try to get the ball.

Glossary

antennas: flexible rods on the net that help show when the ball goes out of bounds

attack line: the line that divides the front and back zones

back zone: the area between the attack and end lines

block: when players jump up at the net to stop a hard spike from the other team

bump: a pass where the ball contacts the forearms; arms are straight and hands are joined

carries: holds the ball instead of letting it bounce quickly off the fingertips

fault: an illegal move or play called by an official

free zone: the area outside the end lines and side lines

front zone: the court area between the attack line and center line

kills: strong hits that result in points; usually done by spiking the ball

match: a series of three or five games

mesh: fine rope linked together forming a loose kind of screen

rally: a series of hits over the net between teams

rotate: clockwise movement teams make before serving the ball; occurs after a side out is called

serving: hitting the ball overhand or underhand over the net from behind the end line

set: a soft hit with the fingertips that can send the ball high into the air; also called a volley

side out: the call made when the serving team commits a fault, causing it to lose the right to serve

spike: a hard, downward hit made above the net, aimed at the opponent's side of the court

warmup: gentle exercise to get the body ready for stretching and game play

Index

Log on to www.av2books.com

AV² by Weigl brings you media enhanced books that support active learning. Go to **www.av2books.com**, and enter the special code inside the front cover of this book. You will gain access to enriched and enhanced content that supplements and complements this book. Content includes video, audio, web links, quizzes, a slide show, and activities.

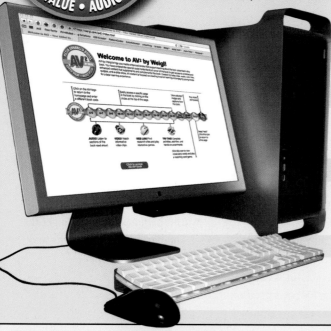

Audio
Listen to sections of the book read aloud.

Video
Watch informative video clips.

Web Link
Find research sites and play interactive games.

Try This!
Complete activities and hands-on experiments.

WHAT'S ONLINE?

Try This! Complete activities and hands-on experiments.	**Web Link** Find research sites and play interactive games.	**Video** Watch informative video clips.	**EXTRA FEATURES**
Pages 6-7 Test your knowledge of volleyball equipment.	**Pages 4-5** Find out more information about the history of volleyball.	**Pages 4-5** View a video about volleyball.	 **Audio** Hear introductory audio at the top of every page.
Pages 8-9 Use this activity to test how well you know the volleyball court.	**Pages 8-9** Learn more about the volleyball court.	**Pages 18-19** View an interview with one of the world's top volleyball players.	**Key Words** Study vocabulary, and play a matching word game.
Pages 12-13 See how well you know volleyball positions.	**Pages 10-11** Learn more about the basics of volleyball.		
Pages 16-17 Write a biography about one of the superstars of volleyball.	**Pages 12-13** Read about volleyball positions.		**Slide Show** View images and captions, and try a writing activity.
Pages 20-21 Play an interactive game.	**Pages 14-15** Learn about playing volleyball indoors and outdoors.		**AV² Quiz** Take this quiz to test your knowledge
Page 22 Test your volleyball knowledge.	**Pages 20-21** Find out more about stretching.		